COOKING HEALTHY

COOKING WITH EGGS AND DAIRY

BY JILLIAN POWELL
WITH RECIPES BY CLARE O'SHEA

rosen publishing's
rosen
central

New York

Published in 2012 by The Rosen Publishing Group Inc.
29 East 21st Street, New York, NY 10010

First Edition

Commissioning Editor: Jennifer Sanderson
Designer: www.rawshock.co.uk
Photographer: Andy Crawford
Illustrator: Ian Thompson
Hand Model: Camilla Lloyd
Proofreader and Indexer: Susie Brooks
Food Consultant: Clare O'Shea

Library of Congress Cataloging-in-Publication Data

Powell, Jillian.
Cooking with eggs and dairy / Jillian Powell, Clare O'Shea.
    p. cm. -- (Cooking healthy)
Includes index.
ISBN 978-1-4488-4843-0 (library binding)
1. Cooking (Eggs)--Juvenile literature. 2. Cooking (Dairy
products)--Juvenile literature. 3. Cookbooks. I. O'Shea, Clare.
II. Title.
TX556.E4P68 2012
641.6'75--dc22

2010039331

Manufactured in China
CPSIA Compliance Information: Batch #S11YA:
For Further Information contact Rosen Publishing, New York, New York at 1-800-237-9932

Photographs:
All photography by Andy Crawford, except: Agripicture Images/
Alamy: 34; ArkReligion.com/Alamy: 35; iStockphoto.com: 9, 16,
21T, 27, 28, 29T, 36, 37, 42, 43 ;Jaubert Bernard/Alamy: 40; Joerg
Boethling/Still Pictures: 17; Nigel Cattlin/Alamy: 18; Ellen Denuto/
Getty Images: 4; Enigma/Alamy: 19; Gallo Images/Getty Images: 20;
Juniors Bildarchiv/Alamy: COVER, 6; Taylor S. Kennedy/
Getty Images: 24; Stockbyte/Getty Images: 8T; 3D4Medical.com/
Getty Images: 11

Contents

Eggs, Dairy Foods, and a Balanced Diet

Eggs and dairy products are found in an enormous range of foods— as ingredients, you may not even know you are eating them! Dairy foods include milk, cream, butter, yogurt, and cheese, which can be eaten as they are or cooked into delicious dishes.

Where Do Eggs and Dairy Foods Come From?

Eggs and dairy foods are the products of animals, usually reared on farms. Most of the eggs we eat come from hens, and cows are the main source of milk. These animals may be farmed intensively indoors or "free range" outdoors. Some farms are organic, creating their produce without using chemicals such as routine drugs or pesticides on crops. Eggs and dairy foods may be bought from local suppliers, or imported from abroad.

Choosing What We Eat

The foods people eat, or their diet, vary around the world, partly depending on the climate and what grows best in particular areas. Personal beliefs and culture also affect our food choices. Many people object to eating meat or fish and instead follow a vegetarian diet. For them, eggs and dairy foods can be an important source of protein. Vegans, however, do not eat dairy foods or eggs since they come from animals. Their diet is based entirely on plant foods.

A Healthy Diet

Our diet is an important part of a healthy lifestyle. There are five main food groups that contain different nutrients that work together to keep the body healthy. These groups are often shown on a "food plate," where you can see the proportions in which they should be eaten (see page 5).

Added to these food groups is water. We need about six to eight glasses of water each day to keep our bodies healthy.

Mozzarella cheese makes a tasty topping for pizza.

The Food Plate

Fruit and vegetables: Full of vitamins and minerals, these foods protect our body and reduce the risk of heart disease, stroke, and some cancers. The fiber in them helps to bulk up our food and keep our digestive system healthy. Fruit and vegetables are low in fat, so they fill us up without unnecessary calories.

Carbohydrates: These provide us with energy. Starchy carbohydrates, which include grains and cereals, should make up about 30 percent of the food we eat. Starchy carbohydrates are an important source of energy for sportsmen and women because they release the energy slowly, keeping the body going for longer.

FRUIT AND VEGETABLES

CARBOHYDRATES

PROTEIN

FATS

MILK AND DAIRY

Protein: This builds and repairs our bones, muscles, skin, hair, and tissues. Meat, fish, eggs, and legumes, which provide body-building proteins, should make up about 15 percent of our total daily diet.

Fats: These keep us warm and can also be stored in the body for energy. Foods that are high in saturated fats (fats from animal sources) or sugar, such as cakes, cookies, and chips, should be eaten only in small amounts (about 8 percent of our total diet). Fats found in oily fish, olives, and nuts and seeds are called unsaturated fats. Saturated fats are linked to an increased risk of heart disease. Eating unsaturated fats is a healthier alternative.

Dairy: Dairy products include milk, butter, yogurt, and cheese. They are packed with nutrients, such as calcium, magnesium, Vitamin K, zinc, and protein, and help to build strong bones and teeth. Yogurt is full of good bacteria and improves our immune system and digestive health. It is best to eat cheese in moderation because it can be high in saturated fat.

FOOD FACTS

Teenage boys need 1,000 milligrams (mg) of calcium a day and girls need 800 mg a day. A glass of milk (5 fl. oz. (150 ml)) provides 234 mg of calcium, and 1.5 oz. (40 g) of Cheddar cheese provides 288 mg.

Looking at Eggs

Eggs are an important and versatile part of our diet. Cooked on their own, they are a naturally healthy food—and they can also be used to make a variety of less healthy treats.

Where Do Eggs Come From?

Birds, fish, and animals such as turtles and crocodiles, lay eggs to produce their young. Eggs that are fertilized by a male can grow and hatch into babies. We eat eggs that have not been fertilized—mainly hens' eggs, but also duck, goose, and quails' eggs. Fish eggs, such as salmon and cod roe and caviar (sturgeon eggs), are also edible and are served as a delicacy in some parts of the world.

Which Eggs to Buy?

You might notice a variety of hen eggs on the supermarket shelves. Eggs come in different sizes and colors, depending on the type of chicken that laid them. They may also be free range or factory farmed. Many people object to the conditions in factory farms, where hens are kept in cages instead of being allowed to roam free. This also affects the eggs' flavor, since these chickens are raised on a controlled diet.

Why Eat Eggs?

Eggs contain a high amount of protein and many important vitamins and minerals. Proteins, which we need to grow and repair our bodies, are made from amino acids. The body can make some amino acids but it must take others (which are called essential amino acids) from our food. The protein in eggs contains all the essential amino acids that we need for a healthy body. Eggs are also rich in Vitamin A, which is important for healthy eyes, skin, and bones, Vitamin B12, which is needed for the blood and nervous system, and Vitamin D, needed for strong bones and teeth. The minerals in eggs include iodine, phosphorus, calcium, and iron—all of which are essential for a healthy body.

 Scratching around in soil or straw is natural behavior for chickens.

Eggs are traditionally sold by the dozen (12) or half dozen (6).

FOOD FACTS

Eggs are such a good source of protein that other protein-rich foods are measured against them. One egg provides about as much protein as 25 grams of lean meat, fish, or poultry.

Food	Protein rating
Eggs (whole)	100
Eggs (whites)	88
Poultry	79
Fish	70
Lean beef	69
Cows' milk	60
Peanuts	55
Soybeans	47

Cholesterol

One egg contains about 5 grams of fat (most of which is "healthy" unsaturated fat) and 213 milligrams of cholesterol, mainly in the yolk. Cholesterol is a fatty substance that the body makes naturally and also takes from some foods. Our bodies need some cholesterol, and there are "good" and "bad" types but doctors recommend that we have no more than 300 milligrams a day from our diet because high blood cholesterol can lead to heart disease.

Dishes and Customs

Eggs are a very versatile cooking ingredient and are used in many favorite dishes around the world, from French toast and Spanish omelette to the African dishes of chakchouka (eggs with peppers) and eggs on fried okra. Eggs also play an important part in many food customs that celebrate birth and new life. Easter eggs (painted or chocolate eggs) are a symbol of the resurrection of Christ in the Christian calendar. Muslims in the Middle East give wrapped eggs to newly-wed couples to bring good luck and health. In China, painted eggs are given as gifts when a baby is one month old, to celebrate the new life.

Cooking Eggs

Eggs can be boiled in the shell, poached, fried, scrambled, or baked. They can also be put to many different uses in cooking. Eggs can be whisked up and heated to thicken quiches, custards, and flans, used to bind ingredients together, or painted on pastries to create a glossy glaze.

Timing It Right

As eggs are heated, the proteins in them change. In raw eggs, the proteins form long chains of amino acids curled into a ball. When they are heated, the chains unfold and begin to bind together into a mesh and the egg starts to set, or coagulate. If eggs are cooked for too long or on too high a heat, too many bonds form and the texture becomes rubbery. In general, eggs should be cooked over gentle heat and removed as soon as they are set.

Boiled Eggs

Eggs for boiling should be taken out of the refrigerator and at room temperature before cooking. If they come straight out of the refrigerator, the shells can crack as the water heats. The water should be simmering rather than boiling before you place the egg in it. Soft-boiled eggs will take 3–5 minutes, and hard-boiled eggs 7–10 minutes.

Poached Eggs

Eggs can be poached, out of their shells, in simmering water, or in buttered poaching trays standing in a pan. If you are not using poaching trays, stir the simmering water to create a whirlpool effect, add the egg to the water, and leave for the required time. A runny egg will take 2 minutes, but if you want a firm egg, this will take 4 minutes.

Boiled eggs are a protein-rich breakfast food.

Poached eggs and spinach are ingredients for the Italian dish, eggs Florentine.

Fried eggs are part of a traditional English breakfast, and are usually served with bacon.

Fried Eggs (Sunny-Side Up)
Fried eggs are cracked into hot fat or oil in a frying pan. The eggs should be allowed to settle and begin to go firm before gently lifting the sides and spreading the oil around. The heat can be turned up for a crispy white.

Scrambled Eggs and Omelettes
For scrambled eggs and omelettes, eggs must be beaten or whisked before cooking. Scrambled eggs are stirred into a frying pan of hot, melted butter until they just begin to coagulate. Continual stirring breaks them into creamy lumps.

 KNOW YOUR FOOD

Cool hard-boiled eggs under cold running water to stop the white turning gray.

For omelettes, butter or oil is heated in a frying pan before the beaten eggs are poured in and allowed to cook until almost set. Some cooks add a little milk or water to the eggs before they are added to the pan. You could also add ingredients such as mushrooms and grated cheese to add flavor to the omelette.

Baked Eggs
A simple but tasty way of cooking eggs is to bake them in a hot oven. The egg should be carefully broken into a buttered dish or ramekin, then seasoned and dotted with butter. The dish is then placed in a roasting pan containing enough hot water to come halfway up its sides. Cooking takes about 15–20 minutes at 375°F (190°C).

Binding and Blending
Egg yolks contain emulsifiers—binding agents that help to blend and stabilize other ingredients. This makes eggs useful for thickening sauces and custards and also for binding together ingredients in fish cakes, meat loaves, and burgers.

Raw eggs can be used to blend oil and vinegar or lemon juice to make a creamy mayonnaise. If the ingredients are shaken together to make a simple dressing, they will mix temporarily but separate again because oil is more dense than vinegar. However, when eggs are added, some of the amino acids in the egg stick to the oil and others to the vinegar, holding them together in a smooth blend.

Adding Volume

When egg whites are whisked or beaten, they form a foam of air bubbles. Air becomes trapped between the chains of proteins as they unfold and mesh together. When the mixture is heated, the air bubbles expand and protein in the egg white coagulates around them. This traps the bubbles to give a light and airy texture. Egg whites can be used to puff up soufflés, and make fluffy omelettes, meringues, and mousses. Whole eggs are beaten into cake batters to help produce a springy sponge.

Always use clean utensils when beating egg whites. Avoid using plastic bowls, since traces of grease or oil can spoil fluffy egg white. Once the egg whites have formed soft peaks, use them immediately or they will start to lose air and volume. They should be carefully folded into heavier ingredients, never the other way round.

Glazing and Coating

Eggs can be beaten and brushed onto bread or pastry before baking. As the egg proteins bake, they form a crispy, golden glaze that not only looks attractive, but will also hold toppings such as nuts, seeds, or breadcrumbs in place. Foods for frying, such as fish cakes and chicken breasts, can be coated with a beaten egg and then dipped in breadcrumbs.

Storing and Handling Eggs

Eggs need careful handling and storage. They should always be kept in a refrigerator and used when they are as fresh as possible. Make sure you check the use-by date and avoid using eggs that are dirty or cracked. Once eggs have been cracked, they should be used immediately. Egg whites can be stored in a sealed container in a refrigerator for a few days or frozen for later use.

FOOD FACTS

A beaten egg white can foam up to eight times its original size.

Fresh Eggs

To test how fresh an egg is, put it in a glass of water. A fresh egg will sink; a less fresh egg will stand on its end, and a stale egg will float. This is because as eggs get older, they lose moisture through the shell and take in more air, which makes the air pocket inside bigger and the egg lighter.

Food Safety

It is important to follow food safety rules when using eggs. This is because some raw or lightly cooked eggs may contain harmful bacteria, such as salmonella, which can cause food poisoning. Very young children, pregnant women, and sick

 These eggs are fresh, so they have sunk to the bottom of the bowl. Older eggs will stand on end, or if they are stale they will float.

This is what salmonella bacteria look like when viewed under a microscope.

or elderly people can be more at risk from these bacteria, so they should eat only eggs that are cooked all the way through and avoid eggs with runny yolks. For recipes using raw eggs, such as mayonnaise or ice cream, it is best to use pasteurized eggs. These come frozen or in liquid or powder form. They have been heat treated to kill harmful bacteria.

Technique		Description
	Breaking an egg	Break eggs into a separate bowl before adding to a recipe to avoid getting bits of shell in with other ingredients. Crack the egg in its middle against a bowl. Put your fingers into the center of the crack and pull the two halves apart.
	Separating eggs	Crack the egg over a bowl. Keep the yolk in one half of the shell and then gently tip it into the other half of the shell so that the white falls into the bowl.

Meringues

A perfect summer's dessert, meringues are delicious served with any fruit, whipped cream, or ice cream.

Ingredients
2 egg whites
¼ cup (50 g) superfine sugar
fresh fruit, to serve
heavy cream, whipped, to serve

1. Preheat the oven to 275°F (140°C).

2. Whisk the egg whites until they just start to get stiff.

3. Gradually add the sugar, whisking all the time.

4. When all the sugar is added, the whites should be stiff and form peaks. They should be stiff enough to turn the bowl upside down without them moving.

5. Place waxed paper on a baking sheet. Put the egg whites in a piping bag or use a spoon to make small pyramid shapes of egg whites.

6. Bake the meringues for approximately 1 hour until they are fully dry. When they are cool, they should come off the waxed paper very easily.

7. Whip the cream before serving it with the meringues and fresh fruit.

Bacon and Mushroom Quiche

SERVES: 2 | **PREPARATION TIME: 30 MINUTES** | **COOKING TIME: 50 MINUTES**

This quiche can be eaten hot or cold. It makes a delicious weekend brunch dish and is perfect for a summer picnic.

Ingredients
2 oz. (50 g) bacon
3 mushrooms, sliced
½ cup (125 ml) milk
2 eggs
2 oz. (50 g) Cheddar cheese, grated
1 large tomato, sliced, plus extra
   for serving
sprig of parsley, to serve

For the pastry
¾ cup (100 g) all-purpose flour
3½ tablespoons (50 g) butter
pinch salt
1 tablespoon water

1. Preheat the oven to 375°F (190°C). Grease a 7-in. (18-cm) flan dish.

2. Cut the rind off the bacon and cut the bacon into small pieces. Fry it over medium heat until there is no pink left on it.

3. Add the mushrooms to the pan. Fry them until soft. Set aside the mushrooms and bacon to use later.

4. To make the pastry, rub the butter into the flour and salt with your fingertips until it resembles breadcrumbs (see page 47).

5. Stir in the water with a metal spoon to make a soft dough. If the mixture does not stick together, add a little more water.

6. Roll out the pastry to the same size as the flan dish, then line the dish with the pastry.

7. Put the milk in a pitcher and crack the eggs into it. Beat well to mix.

8. Put the bacon, grated cheese and mushrooms into the flan dish and pour the milk over it and egg mixture.

9. Place the tomato slices over the top of the quiche.

10. Bake for 30–40 minutes until golden brown and firm to touch.

11. Garnish with the parsley and serve hot or cold with slices of fresh tomato.

Buttercup Scrambles

These eggy baskets are perfect for a brunch meal or a weekend breakfast. You can add slices of cherry tomato, too, for extra flavor.

Ingredients

1 stick (125 g) butter
8 slices thin bread
5 eggs
1 tablespoon fresh parsley, chopped
¼ cup plus 1 tablespoon (90 ml) milk
3.5 oz. (100 g) garlic sausage
2 sticks of celery, chopped
2 green onions , trimmed and finely chopped
2 oz. (50 g) Cheddar cheese, grated

1. Preheat the oven to 400°F (200°C).

2. Melt 7 tablespoons (100 g) of the butter and allow it to cool, but not to set.

3. Trim the crusts from the bread and dip each slice in the melted butter to coat evenly.

4. To make the buttercups, use the buttered bread to line 8 deep muffin tins, leaving the corners of each slice of bread uppermost.

5. Bake the cups for 15–20 minutes, until golden.

6. In the meantime, break the eggs into a bowl, then add the parsley and milk and beat with a fork.

7. Cut the sausage into slices. Melt the remaining butter in a pan, add the sausage, and fry until cooked.

8. Add the egg mixture to the pan with the sausages and cook over low heat until it begins to set.

8. Stir in the celery, green onions, and cheese and mix well.

9. When the cups are ready, divide the egg mixture evenly between each cup and serve immediately.

Classic Omelette

SERVES: 1	PREPARATION TIME: 15 MINUTES	COOKING TIME: 7–10 MINUTES

This classic omelette recipe makes a quick and easy meal.

Ingredients
2 eggs
1 tablespoon water
salt and pepper
1 tablespoon vegetable oil
fried mushrooms, to serve

1. Lightly beat the eggs, water, salt, and pepper together in a bowl.

2. Heat the oil in a frying pan over medium heat. Turn up the heat to high.

3. Pour the eggs into the frying pan, tilting the pan as you do this.

4. Allow the uncooked egg to run to the edges, while the center cooks.

5. While the center is still runny, fold over the omelette and place it on a serving plate. Serve with some fried mushrooms.

COOK'S TIP

To make a cheese omelette, add 2 oz. (50 g) grated Cheddar cheese after pouring in the eggs.

French Toast

SERVES: 2	PREPARATION TIME: 20 MINUTES	COOKING TIME: 10 MINUTES

French toast is delicious with fruit, but it can also be served with bacon and grilled tomatoes.

Ingredients
2 eggs
½ teaspoon sugar
½ teaspoon salt
½ cup (120 ml) milk
4–6 slices white bread
1 tablespoon butter
syrup, to serve
fruit, to serve
confectioners' sugar, to serve

1. Break the eggs into a bowl and beat gently.

2. Stir in the sugar, salt, and milk.

3. Place the bread, one slice at a time, into the egg mixture. Turn the bread over so that each slice is covered in egg on both sides.

4. Melt the butter in a frying pan or griddle over medium heat.

5. Place the eggy bread on the griddle and cook until brown underneath. Turn over and cook the other side.

6. Serve with the syrup and fruit and a dusting of confectioners' sugar.

Looking at Dairy Foods

Dairy foods include milk and foods made from milk, such as butter, cream, cheese, ice cream, cream cheese, and yogurt. They add great flavor and variety to our diet—and in the right amounts, they are good for us, too.

Where Do Dairy Products Come From?

Most of the milk we use is produced by cows, but people also use milk from goats, sheep, buffaloes, yaks, and other animals. These animals may be kept on commercial farms with dairies, or in some places, a family may own one or two animals to supply just the milk they need. In dairies and factories, milk is processed in different ways to turn it into a wide range of dairy foods.

Why Eat Dairy Foods?

Milk and dairy foods are an excellent source of protein, potassium, phosphorus, and Vitamins A and D. They are also the richest dietary source of calcium. Calcium is needed to build strong bones and teeth and reduce the risk of diseases, such as osteoporosis, and tooth decay. Some studies show that increasing our intake of calcium, potassium, and phosphorus can lower blood

 Dairy products come in a variety of forms, textures, and flavors.

pressure and so help to keep the heart healthy. Milk is important for babies and children—it helps them to grow and develop healthy bodies with strong muscles, bones, and teeth. It is also a useful food for elderly and sick people, because it is easy to digest.

Milk Fat

Milk and dairy foods contain fat, which we need to keep us warm and give us energy. However, too much saturated fat can make the blood sticky and clog the arteries, leading to heart disease. Milk can be skimmed or semi-skimmed to reduce the fat content. Half-fat and low-fat milk and dairy foods are healthy options because they contain little saturated fat. They have the same amount of protein and calcium as whole or full-fat milk, and most vitamins except Vitamins A and D, which are lost during skimming. Extra milk solids and vitamins are often added to improve the flavor and increase the nutrients in low-fat dairy products. Sometimes, extra sugar is added, too, which is not good for us if eaten in large quantities.

 This water buffalo is being milked by hand in Mumbai. Water buffalo are the chief dairy animals in India.

 FOOD FACTS

We need Vitamin D to help our bodies absorb calcium. Vitamin D is made by the body when the skin is exposed to sunlight. It is also found in dairy products, egg yolks, and fish.

Milk

On its own, milk is one of the most "complete" foods because it is packed with important nutrients. What is more, you do not need to cook it—it tastes good just as it is!

Types of Milk

There are many different types of milk. Most of the milk we use has been pasteurized, which means it has been treated to kill any harmful bacteria or enzymes that might be present in raw milk. Some milk is homogenized—processed to break up the globules of milk fat so the cream does not separate out and the milk stays smooth and uniform.

Milk that is heat-treated (UHT) has a longer shelf life than fresh milk. Milk can also be evaporated or condensed by boiling off the water content to leave concentrated milk solids. Condensed milk may have sugar added to it to sweeten and preserve it. Dried or powdered milk can also be stored for long periods, and mixed with water or added to dry ingredients for cooking.

KNOW YOUR FOOD

Evaporated milk can be whipped and used as a low-fat alternative to cream.

 In 1856, the French scientist Louis Pasteur discovered that heating liquids to high temperatures kills bacteria. This process is called pasteurization, and it protects the purity and flavor of milk. Milk is pasteurized in hygienic plants such as this one.

In many countries, the different colors on milk packaging refer to the fat content of the milk. For example, in many places in the United States, skimmed milk bottles have blue labels, and whole (full-fat) milk has red labels.

Organic milk and milk products come from cows that have grazed on pasture that is free from chemical fertilizers or pesticides.

Why Drink Milk?

Milk contains more than ten important nutrients, including protein, carbohydrate, Vitamin A (for healthy growth, skin, and eyes), B vitamins (which help us to take energy from food and keep the blood and nervous system healthy), Vitamin D (for healthy bones), and important minerals including calcium, potassium, and phosphorus. Milk is the richest dietary source of calcium. A pint of milk a day provides all the calcium we need.

Milk also contains milk sugars, or carbohydrates, called lactose. Some people can be lactose-intolerant, which means that their bodies are unable to digest milk sugars. This is because they have a shortage of the enzyme lactase, made by cells in the small intestine. This enzyme is needed to break down milk sugars so they can be absorbed into the blood. People who

are lactose-intolerant can choose alternatives to dairy products, such as soy or rice milk and spreads and drinks made from these.

Different Milks

Goat and sheep's milk are more easily digested than cow's milk and can often be drunk by those who are lactose intolerant. They are popular in Mediterranean countries, such as Greece, where there is less pasture for grazing cattle. About 15 percent of the world's milk production is from water buffaloes, which are farmed in Southeast Asia, South America, and Italy. This milk is higher in protein and calcium and contains less cholesterol than cow's milk. Dried or powdered milk is used in places where the climate makes the storage and transportation of fresh milk difficult.

FOOD FACTS

It is the proteins (called casein) in milk that reflect light and make milk look white.

Milk can be drunk hot or cold or mixed into drinks such as smoothies, shakes, tea, coffee, and hot chocolate. As a cooking ingredient, milk adds body and makes dishes smooth and creamy.

Milk in Cooking

Milk can be used to make custards, pancakes, waffles, and milky rice or bread puddings. In South America, the popular sweet dulce de leche is made by gently heating milk and sugar to form a rich caramel. Milk can also be used as an ingredient in many savory dishes, including soups, white sauces, and risottos. It may be used to poach fish, or to soak breadcrumbs for meat loaves or burgers.

Storing Milk

Milk should be kept refrigerated and used within three or four days. It should always be kept covered because it can pick up flavors from other foods in a refrigerator, and away from sunlight, which can destroy the vitamin content. Some milk can be frozen, but this can break down the casein proteins and make the milk look "curdled."

Heating Milk

Milk should be used at room temperature for cooking. It should always be heated slowly and gently to avoid burning. This is because when milk is heated, some proteins separate out and settle at the bottom of the pan where they can easily scald. Milk proteins can also cluster on the surface of the milk, forming a skin as water in the milk evaporates. To prevent a skin forming, cover the saucepan with a lid.

 Milk tarts can be flavored with nutmeg or cinnamon like this South African version.

Curdling

When milk is added to soup or other hot dishes, it can curdle. This happens when the casein proteins begin to coagulate and clump together. Too much heat, acid (such as vinegar or lemon juice), and salt can all cause curdling. To avoid it, use whole milk for cooking. The higher fat content makes milk more stable. Remember to heat it through gently and add any salt just before serving.

 Iced coffee, made with chilled milk, is increasingly popular in the summer when it is too warm to drink hot coffee.

Classic White Sauce

MAKES: 300ML | PREPARATION TIME: 1 MINUTE | COOKING TIME: 15 MINUTES

White sauces are used as a basis for cheese sauces and other sauces such as béchamel sauce.

Ingredients
1¾ tablespoons (25 g) butter
¼ cup (25g) all-purpose flour
1¼ cup (300 ml) milk

1. Melt the butter in a saucepan.

2. Blend in the flour and cook over low heat, stirring all the time with a wooden spoon. The mixture will become a thick lump, which is called a roux.

3. Add a little milk and beat vigorously until the mixture leaves the sides of the pan. Add a little more milk and beat again. Allow the milk to boil and thicken, then add more milk. Continue to do this until all the milk has been used.

4. When all the milk has been added, heat the sauce to boiling and allow to simmer for 5 minutes.

 COOK'S TIP

You can add cheese, parsley, or chopped garlic—or a combination of all three—to add flavor to the sauce.

Lemon Crêpes (Pancakes)

SERVES: 2   PREPARATION TIME: 20 MINUTES   COOKING TIME: 15–20 MINUTES

You can make these thin and tangy French pancakes any time of the day or night! They make a delicious breakfast or an appetizing snack.

Ingredients
1 egg
1 cup (250 ml) milk
¾ cup (100 g) all-purpose flour
1 tablespoon superfine sugar
2 tablespoons vegetable oil
juice 1 lemon

1. Break the egg into a pitcher and add the milk. Mix well.

2. Put the flour in a bowl, add the milk mixture, and whisk to make a smooth batter. Pour the batter back into the pitcher.

3. Heat a little of the oil in a small frying pan over medium heat.

4. When the oil is hot, pour in just enough batter to cover the bottom of the pan.

5. Cook the pancake until the bottom is golden brown. Turn the pancake over and cook the other side.

6. When the pancake is cooked, put it on a plate, sprinkle with lemon juice and sugar, and roll it up.

7. Return the pan to the heat, add a little oil, and when it is hot, add more batter and cook the next pancake in the same way. Continue to do this until all the batter has been used.

COOK'S TIP

Make a hot chocolate sauce and pour this over the crêpes instead of lemon and sugar.

Bread and Butter Pudding

SERVES: 3–4	PREPARATION TIME: 20 MINUTES	COOKING TIME: 40 MINUTES

This winter pudding can be served with custard or cream—but it is so delicious that you may just want to eat it as it is!

Ingredients

1¾ tablespoons (25 g) butter
3 slices bread, without crusts
2 oz. (50 g) dried fruit
1 tablespoon sugar
1½ cups (350 ml) milk
2 eggs, beaten
pinch nutmeg
light cream, to
  serve

1. Preheat the oven to 350°F (180°C).

2. Grease an ovenproof dish with a little of the butter. Use the rest to spread on the bread. Cut the bread into triangles.

3. Put a layer of bread into the dish and sprinkle with some of the fruit and sugar. Continue with these layers until all the bread, fruit, and sugar has been used—you should end with a layer of bread.

4. Warm the milk in a saucepan, but do not let it boil. Add the milk to the eggs and mix well.

5. Pour the milk and egg mixture over the bread. Sprinkle the pudding with nutmeg and set it aside for 10 minutes.

6. Bake in the oven for 30–40 minutes, until golden brown and set. Serve with cream.

Rice Pudding

SERVES: 3–4	PREPARATION TIME: 10 MINUTES	COOKING TIME: 2 HOURS

This hearty pudding is an old favorite. It is everything a pudding should be—sweet, filling, and mouth-wateringly good!

Ingredients

2 oz. (50 g) pudding rice
¼ cup (50 g) sugar
2¼ cups (500 ml) milk
1 tablespoon (15g)
  butter, diced

1. Preheat the oven to 300°F (150°C).

2. Wash the rice in a sieve under cold running water. Put it in an ovenproof dish and sprinkle it with the sugar.

3. Pour the milk over this and dot with the butter.

4. Bake for about 2 hours until the rice is soft.

COOK'S TIP

Add dates and raisins for a sweeter pudding.

Cheese

There are thousands of different types of cheese. They reflect a world of different flavors and cooking styles, although they all start off in the same way—as milk.

Making Cheese

Cheese can be produced by hand in small dairies or by machines in giant factories. It is made by separating the solid curds from the runny whey in milk. Pasteurized milk is pumped into large vats and warmed, then treated with a bacterial culture. This ferments and flavors the milk and helps it to coagulate or become solid. Animal or vegetable rennet is then added, and enzymes in the rennet separate the thick curds from the runny whey proteins.

To make soft cheeses, such as cottage cheese and cream cheese, the whey is drained off as the curds coagulate. These cheeses are ready to eat within hours or days. To make firm cheeses, the curds are stirred or stirred and heated to remove the whey, then salted and pressed into molds and stored to mature. This can be for several months, depending on the type of cheese. Salt improves the flavor and texture of the cheese and also acts as a preservative.

 These Swiss cheeses are being carefully stored so that they can ripen or mature.

Unpasteurized Cheese

Some cheeses are made with unpasteurized milk. These include Stilton, Brie, and Camembert cheese. While such cheeses are prized for their flavor, there is a small risk that they might grow harmful bacteria, including listeria. Blue cheeses and soft cheeses that are ripened in the mold, such as Brie or Camembert, should be avoided during pregnancy because listeria could harm the unborn baby.

This range of cheese includes English Cheddar (1), Swiss Emmental (2), Italian Parmesan (3), Dutch Edam (4), French Brie (5), and Greek feta (6).

Cheese from Other Animals

Cheese can also be made from the milk, pasteurized or unpasteurized, of other animals. Goat cheese is made by warming the milk then separating out the curds and whey using rennet. The curds are drained and pressed into round cheeses, which can be stored in cloth and eaten as a soft cheese after a few days or allowed to mature and form a rind in brine. Greek feta is traditionally made from sheep's milk. The milk is curdled with rennet, then the curds are drained and cut into slices (or "feta" in Greek). These are salted and stored for anything from a week to several months in the salty whey or brine. Mozzarella is an Italian cheese traditionally made with water buffalo milk. When the curds have been separated from the whey, they are "spun" by dipping them into hot water so they form long strings. These are kneaded and folded together to make a stretchy elastic ball of cheese that is plunged into cold water then stored in brine or oil.

Feta cheese (1) is made from sheep's milk, mozzarella (2) is made from buffalo milk, and goat cheese (3) is made from the milk of goats.

FOOD FACTS

It takes 4.75 quarts (4.5 L) of milk to make 1 lb. (0.5 kg) of cheese.

Texture and Flavor

The texture, flavor, and nutritional content of a cheese vary according to how it is made, the type of milk it is made from, and differences in the starter culture. Swiss cheeses, such as Gouda and Edam, are made using a culture that produces gas, forming holes in the cheese. Blue cheeses, such as Stilton and Danish blue, have a blue type of mold added. The cheeses are stored, then pierced to make air holes that allow the mold to spread through the cheese. Some cheeses have herbs, fruit, or nuts mixed in to add flavor and texture.

 The gas produced by the culture used to make Emmental gives the cheese its distinctive holes.

Curds, whey, or cream can all be used to make different types of cheese. Mascarpone is an Italian cream cheese that is made from cream fermented by lactic acid. It can be used in pasta sauces, risottos, and desserts. Ricotta (which means "re-cooked") is made from scalded whey. It is like a grainy, thick sour cream. Cottage cheese is a fresh cheese that is traditionally made from curd without using rennet, but with lactic acid as the starter culture. It is similar to South Asian paneer, and Mexican queso blanco.

Cheese Rind

Fresh cheeses have no rind. Soft, ripened cheeses, such as Brie and Camembert, and some goat cheeses have a soft and supple rind. Some rinds form naturally on the cheese as it matures, as with Stilton. Others are "washed rinds" that form when the cheese is washed in beer, brine, or another liquid. Washing helps friendly bacteria to grow, ripening and flavoring the cheese. Cheese can also have edible coatings of nuts, herbs, or peppercorns. Some have inedible rinds of wax, twigs, or cloth.

Camembert has a soft rind. The cheese becomes runny at room temperature.

Why Eat Cheese?

Since cheese is a concentrated form of milk, it is a nutritious food and a rich source of protein and calcium in the diet. Some cheeses are high in saturated fats, so they should be eaten in moderation. Full-fat cheeses include firm cheeses, such as Cheddar and Parmesan, and some soft cheeses, including mascarpone, which can have nearly 50 percent fat content. Cheeses made from skimmed milk have a reduced fat content, but they may be less tasty since the milk fat gives cheese its flavor. Brie is a medium-fat cheese, while low-fat cheeses include cottage cheese and light cream cheese.

Storing Cheese

Cheese should be kept in a refrigerator and removed a short while before serving. Wrap firm cheeses to stop them from drying out and picking up flavors from other foods. Waxed paper or aluminum foil is better than plastic wrap because it allows the cheese to "breathe" without drying out. This is important because the living enzymes and bacteria in cheese need air and moisture to survive. Strong-smelling cheeses, such as Gorgonzola and blue cheeses, should be wrapped and stored in an airtight container so that they do not pass on their flavor to other foods.

 Slice or grate hard cheeses, such as Cheddar, just before you are ready to use them, so that they do not dry out.

Serving Cheese

Fresh cheeses, such as cottage cheese, ricotta, and mascarpone, should be kept chilled and used straight from the refrigerator. Some semisoft cheeses, including feta and mozzarella, are best stored in a container filled with water or brine to keep them moist. Serve firm cheeses at room temperature to get the full flavor. Ripened cheeses, including Camembert and Brie, should be taken out of the refrigerator a few hours before use.

FOOD FACTS

Cheese can be a useful source of protein, calcium, and Vitamin B12 in vegetarian diets, but vegans and some vegetarians will not eat cheese made with animal rennet, which is extracted from the stomach of calves.

Cooking with Cheese

Cheese is a tasty and versatile ingredient that can be eaten in snacks and sandwiches as well a variety of cooked dishes. Popular examples include macaroni and cheese, scalloped potatoes, pizza toppings, and creamy desserts such as cheesecake.

Cooking Methods

Different types of cheese cook in different ways. This depends largely on the cheese's texture, which may vary from soft and creamy to crumbly or hard and dense. Some firm cheeses, such as Greek halloumi, are suitable for grilling or frying; others break down easily and can be used in baking or sauces. The Swiss cheese Emmental melts smoothly over low heat and makes a delicious fondue (hot cheese dip). Greek feta can be crumbled over salads or into salad dressings.

Hard cheeses, including Cheddar and Parmesan, cook best and melt easily when they are grated, sliced, or shredded.

KNOW YOUR FOOD

Cheese should always be cooked over very low heat, because too high a temperature can make it tough and rubbery.

 Grating cheese makes it easy to spread as a topping. Mozzarella cheese is grated and sprinkled over pizza bases.

Cheese Dishes

Grated hard cheese can be baked with onions and other ingredients in cheese pies and tarts, or melted into sauces for dishes such as macaroni and cheese, pasta bakes, and lasagna. It can also be mixed with eggs and milk to make cheese soufflés, quiches, and flans, or added to pastry or dough to make cheese straws, scones, or bread. Under the broiler, it makes a crispy "gratin" topping for potato or vegetable dishes. Soft cheeses, such as ricotta, cream cheese, and mascarpone, can be whipped into rich desserts including mousses, cheesecakes, and the Italian tiramisu. Some cheeses are used in salads. For example, mozzarella is traditionally added to tomatoes and avocados to make tricolore, an Italian salad. Feta cheese is teamed with tomatoes, olives, onions, and cucumber to make a Greek salad.

 Cheese is used to make a fondue. Vegetables or bread are dipped into the cheese before eating.

Welsh Rarebit

SERVES: 4   **PREPARATION TIME: 20 MINUTES**   **COOKING TIME: 15–20 MINUTES**

The success of this dish—sometimes mistakenly called Welsh Rabbit—lies in cooking it over low heat until all the cheese has melted.

Ingredients
7.5 oz. (200 g) Cheddar cheese, grated
1¾ tablespoons (25 g) unsalted butter
1 teaspoon English mustard
3 tablespoons milk
salt and pepper
4 slices toast
broiled tomatoes, to serve

1. Put the cheese, butter, mustard, and milk in a saucepan over low heat.

2. Stir the mixture until it is smooth and creamy and coats the back of a wooden spoon. Season to taste.

3. Spoon the cheese onto the toast, then broil until it is golden.

4. Remove from under the broiler and cut each slice of toast in half. Serve immediately with the tomatoes.

Cheese Scones

These scones can be eaten on their own or sliced and spread with butter. They are delicious served as an accompaniment to soup.

Ingredients
1¼ cups (100 g) rolled oats
½ cup plus 2 tablespoons (150 ml) milk
butter, for greasing
1¼ cups (150 g) all-purpose flour, plus extra for dusting
½ teaspoon baking powder
½ teaspoon salt
1 oz. (25 g) Edam cheese, grated

1. Put the oats in a large bowl, pour the milk on top, and leave to soak for 30 minutes.

2. Preheat the oven to 350°F (180°C). Lightly grease a baking sheet.

3. Sieve the flour, baking powder, and salt into the oat mixture. Add the cheese and mix well to make a soft dough.

4. Turn the dough onto a lightly floured surface and knead for 2 minutes (see page 47), until soft and elastic.

5. Roll out the dough to 1 in. (2 cm) thick, then use a cookie cutter to cut out 6 scones.

6. Place the scones on the baking sheet and bake for 20 minutes. Serve warm or cold.

COOK'S TIP

Add crushed garlic and/or chives for extra flavor.

Macaroni and Cheese

| SERVES: 2 | PREPARATION TIME: 20 MINUTES | COOKING TIME: 40 MINUTES |

This baked pasta dish is an old favorite. You can add bacon and green onions for extra flavor.

Ingredients
3.5 oz. (100 g) short-cut macaroni
3.5 oz. (100 g) cheese
¼ cup (25 g) flour
2¼ cups (500 ml) milk
salad, to serve

1. Fill a large saucepan of water and place over medium heat to boil. When the water is boiling, add the macaroni and cook according to the package instructions.

2. In the meantime, preheat the oven to 350°F (180°C).

3. To make the cheese sauce, put the cheese, flour, and milk into a saucepan on low heat. Stir the sauce continuously in a figure of eight movement and gradually increase the heat. The sauce should thicken to coat the back of a wooden spoon.

4. When the macaroni is cooked, drain it before adding it to the cheese sauce. Stir to mix well.

5. Place the macaroni in an ovenproof dish and bake for 20 minutes until it is golden brown. Serve with a side salad.

Cheese-Filled Pancakes

| MAKES: 4 | PREPARATION TIME: 20 MINUTES | COOKING TIME: 10–15 MINUTES |

The spinach in these thin pancakes is packed with iron, and the cheese is calcium rich and low in fat.

Ingredients
¾ cup (100 g) whole-wheat flour
1 egg
2 tablespoons milk
2 tablespoons vegetable oil

For the filling
1 lb. (450 g) spinach
8 oz. (225 g) cottage cheese
salt and pepper

1. Put the flour, egg, and milk into a mixing bowl and mix well to make a smooth batter.

2. Heat a little of the oil in a frying pan. Pour a ladleful of batter into the middle of the pan and spread it until it covers the bottom of the pan.

3. Cook the pancake for 2 minutes and then turn it over and cook the other side. When cooked, place the pancake on a plate. Cook all the pancakes in the same way.

4. Cook the spinach in a frying pan over low heat for 2–3 minutes. Remove the spinach from the heat, drain off any excess water, then add the cottage cheese. Season to taste and mix well.

5. Return the spinach mixture to the heat for 3 minutes.

6. Place spoonfuls of the mixture on each pancake. One at a time, roll up the pancakes and serve.

Savory Appetizers

MAKES: 30 | PREPARATION TIME: 40 MINUTES | COOKING TIME: 20–30 MINUTES

These party snacks look as good as they taste and are sure to impress.

Ingredients
butter, for greasing
1 lb. (450 g) ready-made puff pastry
milk, for brushing
1 bunch fresh chives
2 oz. (50 g) dried cranberries
8 oz. (225 g) cream cheese

1. Preheat the oven to 350°F (180°C). Grease 2 large baking sheets.

2. Roll out the pastry to about ½ in. (1 cm) thick and cut out circles of about 1 in. (2 cm) in diameter.

3. Place the circles on the baking sheets and brush with a little milk.

4. Bake for 10–15 minutes until slightly brown. Remove from the oven and place on a wire rack to cool.

5. In the meantime, finely chop the chives and cut the cranberries in half.

6. Mix the cream cheese with the chives and place teaspoons of the mixture on each pastry base.

7. Top with the dried cranberries and serve.

Strawberry Cheesecake

SERVES: 6 | PREPARATION TIME: 40 MINUTES | CHILLING TIME: 3 HOURS

This cheesecake does not need baking, making it quick and easy to make.

Ingredients
7.5 oz. (200 g) graham crackers
7 tablespoons (100 g) butter
½ cup (120 ml) heavy cream
1 teaspoon confectioners' sugar
8 oz. (225 g) cream cheese
½ cup (120 ml) strawberry yogurt
3.5 oz. (100 g) fresh strawberries, stems removed

1. To make the base, put the cookies into a plastic bag and, using a rolling pin, crush them until they resemble fine breadcrumbs.

2. Melt the butter in a saucepan over medium heat. Remove from the heat and add the cracker crumbs. Stir well.

3. Spread the graham cracker mixture over the base of an 8 in. (20 cm) cake pan.

4. To make the filling, whisk the heavy cream and confectioners' sugar together until they make a mousse-like mixture.

5. Fold the cream cheese into the cream. Fold the yogurt into the cream mixture.

6. Pour the filling over the base and leave in the refrigerator to set for about 1 hour.

7. Take the cake out and decorate with the strawberries. Return the cake to the refrigerator and allow to set for a further 2 hours.

8. Remove from the refrigerator and serve.

Mozzarella Cheese Pizza

SERVES: 2 | **PREPARATION TIME: 40 MINUTES** | **COOKING TIME: 20–30 MINUTES**

You cannot go wrong with this mozzarella pizza—it is easy to make and delicious to eat.

Ingredients

1½ cups (200 g) bread flour, plus extra for sprinkling
1½ teaspoons dried yeast
1 teaspoon salt
½ cup (125 ml) warm water
1 tablespoon vegetable oil, plus extra for greasing

For the topping

2 tomatoes
1 garlic clove, peeled and finely chopped
3 sprigs fresh basil
8 oz. (225 g) mozzarella cheese

1. Preheat the oven to 400°F (200°C).

2. Place the flour, yeast, and salt in a large mixing bowl. Make a well in the middle (see page 47).

3. Place the water in a pitcher and add the oil. Pour the liquid into the well and mix to make a soft dough.

4. Turn the dough out onto a lightly floured surface and knead for 10 minutes (see page 47).

5. Roll out the dough into a round shape and place on a greased baking sheet. Cover with plastic wrap and leave in a warm place to rise for 20 minutes.

6. In the meantime, slice the tomatoes and grate the cheese. Tear the basil into small pieces.

7. When the base is ready, bake it in the oven for 5 minutes. Remove from the oven and add the tomato, cheese, garlic, and basil.

8. Bake the pizza for 20 minutes until golden brown. Serve immediately.

COOK'S TIP

Add some salami or pepperoni slices for a meatier pizza.

Butter and Cream

Butter is made using the cream from cow, sheep, or buffalo milk. It is a useful form of fat for cooking, adding a rich flavor to all kinds of sweet and savory dishes.

Making Butter

To make butter, the cream is skimmed from the milk and pasteurized to destroy any harmful enzymes or bacteria. The cream is then churned until the fat globules separate out from the runny buttermilk and begin to stick together as grains or granules of butter. Next, the butter is drained and mixed with water until a smooth texture is achieved. Some butter has salt added to it. It can also have air or nitrogen gas whipped through it to make it spreadable at cold temperatures.

The Good and Bad in Butter

Butter contains protein, calcium, phosphorus, and Vitamins A, D, and E. Full-fat butter is about 80–82 percent milk fat, 16–17 percent water, and 1–2 percent milk solids. Salted butter contains about 3 percent salt, and slightly salted butter around 1 percent. Butter is high in saturated fats, so it should be eaten in moderation. For low-fat diets, butter is available with a reduced fat content. However, "light" or reduced-fat butters are not suitable for frying or baking, because they contain more water and are less stable when heated.

 FOOD FACTS

It takes 2.4 gallons (9 liters) of whole milk to produce 1 pound (0.45 kg) of butter. Salt adds flavor and gives the butter a longer shelf life.

 In this dairy, butter is being shaped by hand using a traditional butter pat.

Cooking with Butter

Butter can be used for spreading, frying, sautéing, and broiling. It is also used to grease pans or dishes to prevent cakes and bread sticking and as a glaze for pies. Butter can be flavored with garlic, mustard, or herbs to use with fish or meat dishes. In baking, it adds a melt-in-the-mouth quality to pastry, cakes, cookies, and pies. Butter can also be added to hollandaise, beurre blanc (a light, buttery sauce), and other sauces to give a glossy, smooth texture and a rich taste.

Clarified Butter

To make clarified butter, butter is heated to boiling point so that the water content evaporates and the milk solids settle. This leaves a pure, clear liquid fat. In India, the clarified butter, called ghee, is made from buffalo milk. It is widely used in Indian cooking for dishes such as dhal and curries and to make traditional sweets. In some Hindu ceremonies, statues of gods are washed in ghee and it is also thrown into altar fires or used to light holy lamps during festivals.

 This woman is cooking with ghee for a festival in honor of a Hindu spiritual leader, Guru Tegh.

Buttermilk

Buttermilk can be produced by fermenting the runny whey left behind after churning butter. It can also be made by adding a bacterial culture to skimmed milk. Buttermilk has a slightly sour, acidic taste and is a useful ingredient when baking quick breads and scones.

KNOW YOUR FOOD

To stop butter burning, cook it over low heat and combine with a little oil or sprinkle a few grains of salt in the pan before heating.

Cream

To produce cream, milk is heated and spun until the globules of fat separate out. These are skimmed off, then cooled and pasteurized, sterilized, or heat-treated to make long-life UHT cream. Cream is graded by the amount of butterfat it contains. Thick clotted cream can contain up to 55 percent butterfat. Heavy cream contains 40 percent or more, and whipping cream 30 percent or more. Light cream contains at least 18 percent butterfat, and half-and-half, at least 10.5 percent. The higher the percentage of butterfat, the more fattening the cream!

Sour Cream

Cream can have a bacterial culture added to make sour cream or crème fraiche—a thick cream with a sharp flavor. Sour cream is a useful ingredient in soups, stews, cakes, and cheesecakes and makes a tasty topping for fruit, desserts, or baked potatoes. It can also be used as a marinade before cooking, since its slight acidity tenderizes meat and holds seasonings in place.

Types of cream	
	Light cream
	Heavy cream
	Sour cream

FOOD FACTS

We should not eat too much cream, because it is high in saturated fats. A tablespoon of heavy cream contains about 25 grams of fat.

 Sour cream and chives make a tasty topping for baked potatoes.

Scones with jam and clotted cream are part of a traditional tea served in the southwest of England.

Cooking with Cream

Cream can be used to make a huge range of sweet dishes, including the Italian dessert panna cotta, crème caramel, fruit fools, and mousses. It is also used to make creamy sauces for meat or pasta and stews such as goulash. Thicker creams with a higher fat content, such as heavy cream and crème fraiche, are best for thickening sauces since they are more stable and less likely to curdle or separate when heated. Cream can be "scalded" (heated almost to boiling point) to make crème brûlée and ice cream. Whipping cream can be whisked into sauces to add richness, or folded into cakes or mousses for a light texture. It is also delicious served with fruits, as in traditional English strawberries and cream.

COOK'S TIP

It is easier to whisk whipping cream when the cream and bowl are cold, because the fat globules hold together. Stop whisking as soon as the cream stands up in soft peaks.

Storing Cream

Cream should be stored in the refrigerator and used within a few days once opened. Like milk, cream should be kept covered to stop it picking up flavors from other foods.

Chocolate-Chip Cookies

MAKES: 6   PREPARATION TIME: 40 MINUTES   COOKING TIME: 20-30 MINUTES

These cookies are perfect for dunking in a cup of tea or a glass of ice-cold milk.

Ingredients
1 cup (125 g) all-purpose flour, plus extra for sprinkling
7 tablespoons (100 g) butter
2 tablespoons superfine sugar
1 tablespoon beaten egg
½ teaspoon baking powder
3.5 oz. (100 g) milk chocolate chips

1. Preheat the oven to 350°F (180°C). Line a cookie sheet with waxed paper and sprinkle some flour over it.

2. Cream the sugar and butter to make a smooth, creamy mixture (see page 47).

3. Add the egg and mix well.

4. Sieve the flour and baking powder over the butter mixture. Add the chocolate chips and stir well.

5. Make 6 ball shapes out of the dough and place on the cookie sheet. Press down on the balls to flatten them into a cookie shape.

6. Bake for 20 minutes. Remove from the oven but leave on the baking sheet for 5 minutes before allowing to cool on wire rack.

Chocolate Truffles

MAKES: 30   PREPARATION TIME: 20-30 MINUTES   COOKING AND CHILLING TIME: 2 HOURS

Truffles are incredibly addictive, and these are no exception!

Ingredients
½ cup (120 ml) heavy cream
10 oz. (300 g) milk chocolate
3½ tablespoons (50 g) butter
4 shortbread cookies, roughly crumbled
3 oz. (90 g) dried fruit
zest of 1 orange
cocoa powder, for rolling

1. Put the cream into a small saucepan and heat to boiling. Remove from the heat.

2. Put the chocolate and butter into a bowl and place over a saucepan of boiling water until melted.

3. Add the cream, cookies, dried fruit, and orange zest to the chocolate. Stir well. Place in the refrigerator for 1 hour.

4. Use a teaspoon to scoop out the truffle mixture and form it into small balls.

5. Roll each ball in the cocoa powder before placing it in a foil candy cups. Leave in refrigerator to set.

COOK'S TIP

Try dipping the truffles in melted white chocolate instead of rolling them in cocoa powder.

Crème Brûlée

SERVES: 6 | **PREPARATION TIME: 20 MINUTES** | **COOKING AND CHILLING TIME: 7 HOURS 30 MINUTES**

This traditional French dessert is popular around the world. The individual dishes make it perfect for a more formal dinner.

Ingredients
3¼ cups (750 ml) light cream
6 egg yolks
1 level teaspoon superfine sugar
1 tablespoon vanilla extract
2 teaspoons light brown sugar

1. Put the cream in a bowl over a pan of simmering water (see page 47).

2. In another bowl, beat the egg yolks with the superfine sugar and the vanilla extract.

3. When the cream is warm, stir in the egg mixture and cook until the cream has thickened enough to coat the back of a wooden spoon.

4. Pour the mixture into small dishes or ramekins, and allow to chill for 4 hours.

5. Sprinkle the light brown sugar over the top of the puddings.

6. Put the crème brûlées on a tray of ice cubes and place under a hot broiler until the sugar melts.

7. Put the puddings back in the refrigerator and chill for a further 3 hours before serving.

COOK'S TIP

Berries, such as blueberries, strawberries, and raspberries, can be served with this dessert.

Yogurt

Yogurt is made from milk that has been pasteurized and fermented by adding a bacterial culture. We can buy yogurt ready-to-eat in many flavors, but it is also a healthy and versatile cooking ingredient.

Making Yogurt

Yogurt can be made from whole, skimmed, or dried milk—from cows, goats, sheep, or even buffaloes. When bacteria are added to milk, they produce lactic acid, which turns the lactose or milk sugars into lactic acid. Lactic acid breaks down proteins in the milk, making it coagulate and thicken. This process also gives yogurt its tangy, sharp, or slightly sour taste.

Differences in the type of milk, the starter culture, and the way the yogurt is fermented produce many different varieties including set, stirred, frozen, and drinking yogurt. Some yogurt is heat-treated to prolong its shelf life, but this kills many of the friendly bacteria found in live or bio yogurts.

Yogurt for Health

Yogurt is a good source of protein, calcium, and Vitamins B6 and B12. All yogurts contain the harmless bacteria *Lactobacillus bulgaricus* and *Streptococcus thermophilus*. Live yogurts have added "friendly" bacteria that can boost the body's immune system, keep the digestive system healthy, and fight stomach bugs.

Fat Content

Yogurt varies in fat content. Thick, creamy yogurts made from whole milk, sometimes with cream added, have 3–4 percent fat. Some Greek-style or set yogurts are especially thick and creamy and can contain 10 percent fat. They should be eaten in moderation. Low-fat yogurts have up to 2 percent fat, and fat-free yogurts have less than 0.5 percent fat.

 Yogurt is sold in individual cups for convenience. Some cups, such as this one, are made from glass so that they can be recycled.

Types of Yogurt

Set yogurt: These yogurts ferment in the cups and set into a firm, jellylike texture. Some are flavored, others are natural but have a fruit layer in the bottom of the cup.

Bio yogurt: These yogurts have "friendly" bacteria, such as *Lactobacillus acidophilus* and *Bacillus bifidus*, added to them. They usually have a milder, less acidic taste than non-bio varieties. They can be flavored with fruit, such as strawberries.

SET YOGURT

BIO YOGURT

FLAVORED YOGURT

NATURAL YOGURT

Flavored yogurt: These yogurts have been flavored with whole fruit, fruit purée, or syrup or other flavorings, such as chocolate, coffee, or nuts. Although low-fat varieties of flavored yogurts are available, they are often higher in sugar than natural yogurt.

Natural yogurt: These yogurts have had no flavors added and they can be sharp or mild, runny, creamy, or firm and set. The smoothest and creamiest varieties are often higher in fat and calories.

FOOD FACTS

Some people who are lactose-intolerant can eat yogurt, because the active cultures produce the enzyme lactase, which helps the body to break down and digest milk sugars.

Yogurt can be used as a low-fat replacement for many other dairy products in cooking. It works well in soups, sauces, curries, and stews, as well as creamy puddings.

Yogurt Dishes

Natural yogurt can be used as a topping for desserts, cereals, and baked potatoes or mixed with herbs or spices to make dips or side dishes. In Indian cooking, a raita made with yogurt, herbs, and cucumber is often served alongside curried dishes because it cools the flavors of chilies and other hot spices. In Greece, the popular dish tzatziki is made from yogurt mixed with cucumber, garlic, oil, and vinegar. The slight acidity of yogurt also makes it a useful marinade that tenderizes meat. It can be added to pasta sauces, stews, or curries, too, and used in baking cakes, scones, and quick breads.

Yogurt as an Ingredient

Yogurt is an excellent substitute for heavy cream, sour cream, or crème fraiche because it has a similar smooth taste and texture. It can also be used to replace milk, butter, or oil in baking. As an ingredient, it can make baked goods fluffy and moist, and reduce calories and fat content. It may also be combined with baking soda to help scones and cakes rise. Some recipes use yogurt as a low-fat alternative to cream cheese. Mixing yogurt with lemon juice or vinegar makes a light, refreshing salad dressing.

 The cool, tangy taste of natural yogurt compliments hot, spicy curries.

Natural yogurt served with chopped fresh fruit makes a healthy, low-fat dessert that is bursting with vitamins and minerals.

Handling and Heating

Yogurt should always be handled and heated gently, because over-mixing or cooking at too high a temperature can make it curdle or separate and can also destroy friendly bacteria. To stop yogurt separating, add it at the end of cooking time to soups and sauces, and fold it in gently until just heated through. Yogurt can also be mixed with a little cornstarch or all-purpose flour before adding it to a hot dish, since this will help to prevent curdling.

Storing Yogurt

Yogurt should be stored in a refrigerator and used by the use-by date or within a few days of opening. Some yogurts can be frozen in their cups for about two months. They should be completely thawed before eating.

KNOW YOUR FOOD

Do not use aluminum or copper pans for cooking yogurt since the acidic content can react with the metal.

FOOD FACTS

As natural yogurt gets older, it becomes sharper in taste. This is because it can go on fermenting, increasing acidity.

Banana Frozen Yogurt

SERVES: 4　　**PREPARATION TIME: 30 MINUTES**　　　　**CHILLING TIME: 1 HOUR**

This frozen yogurt is lower in fat than ice cream, but it tastes just as good!

Ingredients
3 ripe bananas
2 cups (450 g) low-fat natural
　yogurt
2 nectarines, to serve

1. Peel and mash the bananas in a large bowl.

2. Gradually add the yogurt and beat well to make a smooth, creamy mixture.

3. Pour the mixture into a freeze-proof container with a lid. Cover and freeze for 30 minutes.

4. Tip the mixture back into the bowl and whisk for 2 minutes.

5. Return the mixture back to the freeze-proof container, cover and freeze for another hour.

6. Remove from the freezer and whisk again before returning to the freezer until set. Each time you whisk it, the mixture should be smoother and creamier.

7. When ready to serve, halve the nectarine, remove the pit, and slice each half in half again.

8. Place nectarine pieces around scoops of the frozen yogurt to serve.

COOK'S TIP

Swap the banana for ripe mango or use a combination of the two.

Cucumber Raita

SERVES: 4 | PREPARATION TIME: 20 MINUTES | COOKING TIME: NO COOKING

Raita is perfect for cooling down a hot curry or for dipping poppadams (Indian flat bread).

Ingredients
1 cup (250 ml) natural yogurt
½ cucumber
2 sprigs fresh cilantro, plus extra for garnishing
1 teaspoon black pepper
pinch chili powder

1. Pour the yogurt into a bowl and beat it.

2. Grate the cucumber and finely chop the cilantro.

3. Add the cucumber, cilantro, pepper, and chili powder to the yogurt and mix well. Pour into a bowl to serve.

COOK'S TIP

Try using a chopped, roasted eggplant instead of cucumber.

Cooking with Yogurt

Blueberry Muffins

MAKES: 12 MUFFINS | PREPARATION TIME: 20 MINUTES | COOKING TIME: 20 MINUTES

Blueberry muffins are always popular as a brunch-time treat. They are best eaten on the day they are made.

Ingredients
7 tablespoons (100 g) butter
2½ cups (300 g) flour
½ teaspoon baking powder
½ teaspoon salt
2 eggs
¼ cup plus 2 tablespoons (75 g) superfine sugar
2 tablespoons natural yogurt
3.5 oz. (100 g) blueberries

1. Preheat the oven to 350°F (180°C). Place 12 baking cups in a muffin tin.

2. Melt the butter in a pan, then remove it from the heat.

3. In the meantime, sieve together the flour, baking powder, and salt in a large mixing bowl.

4. Beat the eggs, then add them with the sugar and yogurt to the butter. Mix well.

5. Add the butter mixture to the sifted flour and stir well to make a smooth batter.

6. Add the blueberries and mix well.

7. Place spoonfuls of the batter in the baking cups and bake for 20 minutes until slightly brown.

8. Remove from the oven and serve.

Glossary

amino acids parts of food that make up proteins and help to break them down when food is being digested

bacteria tiny living organisms; some are helpful in the body; others can be harmful

bacterial culture harmless bacteria, used to start fermentation

béchamel a white sauce made with butter, flour, and milk

buttermilk the liquid left after churning butter

carbohydrate a nutrient that gives the body energy

cholesterol a substance made by the body and found in some foods; some types of cholesterol are good for us; others can be harmful

coagulate to thicken into a semisolid or solid mass

curd the solid part of milk, mainly casein proteins

digestive system parts of the body that work together to process food

emulsifier a substance that breaks down fat so that it can dissolve in water

enzyme a chemical agent that changes food into substances that our bodies can absorb

ferment to bring about change so that sugars turn into carbon dioxide and alcohol

fiber the bulky part of food, known as roughage, that is needed for digestion

glaze to give a glossy coating

goulash a type of meat and vegetable stew

immune system the body's natural defenses, which fight off infections and diseases

lactic acid a chemical compound found in sour milk

lactose milk sugars

legumes the seeds of pod-bearing plants, such as beans, which can be dried and used as food

milk solids the solid part left when water has been evaporated from milk

mineral a substance, such as iron, that is found in the soil and the foods we eat

nutrient any part of a food that gives the body energy or the goodness it needs to grow and stay healthy

osteoporosis a bone disease in which the bones become brittle and more likely to break

pasteurized treated by pasteurization to kill harmful bacteria

preservative a chemical substance that is added to food to make it last longer

protein a nutrient that helps the body to grow and repair itself

ramekin a small baking dish

rennet an animal or vegetable substance that contains enzymes to curdle milk in cheese-making

salmonella a harmful type of bacteria that can cause sickness

saturated fat a type of fat that is harmful to the body because it builds up in the arteries and causes heart disease

skimmed thinned by removing cream from the surface

sterilized treated to kill bacteria

tenderize to make meat tender, or easy to chew, by breaking down its tough fibers

vats large tanks

vitamin a special substance found in food, which the body needs in tiny amounts to stay healthy

whey the watery part of milk

Food Safety

Sticking to some simple rules can help you avoid food poisoning and other kitchen dangers.

1. Clean all your work surfaces before you start cooking.

2. If you have long hair, tie it back away from your face.

3. To avoid a serious injury, always wear shoes in the kitchen.

4. Wash your hands well with soap and warm water before you start to cook. Wash them after handling any raw meat, poultry, or fish.

5. Read through the recipe you are cooking before you start. Check that you have all the equipment and ingredients that you will need.

6. Check the use-by dates on all food.

7. Wash all fruit and vegetables under cold, running water.

8. When preparing food, keep it out of the refrigerator for the shortest time possible. Generally, you should not leave food out for longer than 2 hours.

9. Use a different cutting board and knife to prepare meat, chicken, and fish from the one you use for preparing fruit and vegetables.

10. Never serve undercooked food, ensure that any meat, fish, and chicken is cooked all the way through.

11. Replace used dish towels regularly with clean, dry ones to avoid the spreading of bacteria.

 KNOW YOUR FOOD

Useful Information
These abbreviations have been used:
lb.—pound   **oz.**—ounce
ml—milliliter   **g**—gram
cm—centimeter   **mm**—millimeter

1 teaspoon = 5 milliliters
1 tablespoon = 15 milliliters

All eggs are medium unless stated.

Cooking temperatures:
To figure out where the stove dial needs to be for high, medium, and low heat, count the marks on the dial and divide them by three. The top few are high, the bottom few are low, and the in-between ones are medium.

Useful Techniques

Kneading
Place the dough on a lightly floured surface. Press down on the dough with the palm of your hand, then fold the dough over itself and press down again. Continue to do this until the dough is soft and elastic.

Double Boiling
By placing a bowl over a saucepan of boiling water, cream and more delicate ingredients cook slowly enough to ensure that they do not burn.

Making a Well
To make a well in a mixture of dry ingredients, use a spoon to push the ingredients away from the center of the bowl. You should end up with the ingredients on the outer edges of the bowl, and a gap or "well" in the middle.

Creaming
When butter is at room temperature, put it with the required sugar into a bowl. Mix them together until they become a pale yellow, creamy color.

Rubbing In
Use your fingertips to "squash" the butter into the flour—the flour will look lumpy. Continue to rub in the butter until the flour resembles breadcrumbs.

Index

Further Reading

Eat Smart: Milk and Dairy
by Louise Spilsbury (Heinemann Library, 2009)

Meat, Fish, and Eggs
by Susan Martineau and Hel James (Smart Apple Media, 2009)

Yum: Your Ultimate Manual for Good Nutrition
by Daina Kalnins, (Lobster Press, 2008)

Web Sites

Due to the changing nature of Internet links, Rosen Publishing has developed an online list of Web sites related to the subject of this book. This site is regularly updated. Please use this link to access this list: http://www.rosenlinks.com/cook/ced

12|16 ④ 1|16

12|16 ④ 1|16